The Kew Gardens CHILDREN'S COOKBOOK

First published in Great Britain in 2016 by Wayland

ISBN: 978 0 7502 9819 3

10 9 8 7 6 5 4 3 2 1

Printed in China

Wayland
An imprint of
Hachette Children's Group
Part of Hodder & Stoughton
Carmelite House
50 Victoria Embankment
London EC4Y 0DZ

An Hachette UK Company
www.hachette.co.uk
www.hachettechildrens.co.uk

Royal Botanic Gardens, Kew
Richmond
Surrey
TW9 3AB, UK
www.kew.org

Managing Editor: Victoria Brooker
Cover and book designer: Lisa Peacock
Inside design concept: Anita Mangan
Illustrator: Sara Mulvanny
Photography at Kew: Thom Hudson
Food photography: Ian Garlick

Disclaimer
The website addresses (URLs) included in this book were
valid at the time of going to press. However, it is possible
that contents or addresses may have changed since the
publication of this book. No responsibility for any such
changes can be accepted by either the authors, the Royal
Botanic Gardens, Kew, or the Publisher.

The Publishers, the authors and the Royal Botanic Gardens,
Kew cannot accept any legal responsiblity or liability for
accidents or damage arising from the use of any items
mentioned in this book or in the carrying out of any of the
projects. Some of the projects and recipes in this book may involve
nuts or seeds. Anyone with a known nut allergy must avoid these.
Adult supervision of children at all times, when gardening, cooking
or carrying out any activity near water, is advised and tools,
garden equipment, and dangerous garden materials such as
fertilisers should not be left where children can access them
easily or use them without adult guidance.

The Kew Gardens CHILDREN'S COOKBOOK

Joe Archer and Caroline Craig

WAYLAND

Royal Botanic Gardens
Kew

Contents

31

42

Introduction

Growing your own food is great fun. It is fascinating to watch the tiny seeds that you have sown turn into delicious fruit and vegetables. After weeks of weeding and watering, you will be the proud owner of some tasty home-grown produce.

Get planting. get cooking

In this book, you'll find out how plants grow and you can follow instructions for how to plant a range of vegetables. Then, once you have harvested your crops, you can follow the recipes and turn them into delicious meals, snacks and desserts. From pesto-pasta with a twist to a chocolate cake with a hidden vegetable ingredient, the recipes will show you some of the easy, yummy ways you can use vegetables in all of your meals.

Your own patch

You don't have to have a large garden to grow your own vegetables. In fact, you don't even need to have a garden at all! Balconies, hanging baskets, window boxes and small pots are suitable for growing crops. Whatever space you have, there's always room to grow plants.

Kew's Kitchen Garden

The Royal Botanic Gardens, Kew is world famous for its scientific work and its beautiful gardens, which are home to over 19,000 different types of plants. It has a kitchen garden too, created on the same site where over 200 years ago produce was grown for the kings, queens and royal households of England. You can visit Kew's Kitchen Garden to see a bountiful range of mouth-watering fruit and vegetables growing all year round.

So enjoy reading this book and get planting, cooking, and eating with your friends and family.

What parts of a plant do we eat?

Let's think about how many different parts of a plant we eat. What's your favourite vegetable? Can you tell if it's a root, a leaf or a flower?

Roots

Plant roots come in different shapes and sizes. Some roots are long, and used by plants to get food from the soil; others are thick and used to store food and nutrients. Carrots, parsnips, turnips, radishes and beetroots are all root vegetables.

Stems

We also eat the stems of many plants, such as asparagus and rhubarb. Although potatoes grow underground, they are actually part of the plant's stem.

Leaves

Some plant leaves, such as lettuce, we eat raw, and others, such as cabbage, we usually cook. Leaves such as chard or spinach can be eaten both raw and cooked.

Flowers

Can you think of any flowers that you can eat? Cauliflower and broccoli are actually tiny flower buds, and if they were left to grow, they would turn into small yellow flowers.

Seeds

Seeds are often contained in a case called a pod. Sometimes we eat the seeds from these pods, such as peas, and sometimes we eat the pod and the seeds, such as French beans or sugarsnap peas.

Fruits

We eat the fruit produced by many plants, such as apples and oranges. But did you know that courgettes, tomatoes, aubergines and pumpkins are all fruits too? Next time you cut open a piece of fruit, have a look at the seeds inside it. All fruits contain seeds.

Bulbs

Finally, we also eat bulbs such as onions and garlic. A bulb is another part of the plant used to store energy. If a bulb was left to grow, it would eventually produce leaves and flowers.

The miracle of a seed

Seeds are an incredible part of nature. Plants produce seeds in many different shapes and sizes, but they all have one thing in common: they can grow into a new plant.

Did you know?

Just like a bank where you keep your money safe, Kew Gardens has its own bank for seeds. The Millennium Seed Bank aims to collect and store the seeds of plants from all over the world. These seeds are kept safe in case the plants are destroyed or lost in their natural home.

Sow the seed

A seed is a plant ready and waiting. Each one has just the right amount of energy to spring into life. This is important to remember when sowing seeds, because if you sow them too deep the first leaves won't have enough energy to break through the soil.

See for yourself

Seeds don't need to be in soil to be able to germinate. Pea seeds can begin to germinate with just water and warmth. Place some pea seeds onto a folded wet paper towel and leave them in a warm place. After a couple of days, you will see that the seeds have soaked up the water and begun to germinate.

What happens when you plant a seed?

Give most seeds warmth and water and, after a few days, they will begin to grow. If you plant a seed in soil, a root will sprout from the bottom that will branch out and grow down into the soil in search of water. A shoot will grow up from the seed in search of light. When it breaks above the surface of the soil, it produces its first small leaves. This process is called germination.

How do plants reproduce?

Plants begin their lives as tiny seeds. When a seed is planted, roots start to grow. Roots take in nutrients and water from the soil, and help to hold the plant in place. A shoot grows up through the soil towards the light. Above ground, the shoot gets bigger and bigger producing leaves and flowers.

Sweet nectar

Soon, flowers appear. Many flowers have brightly coloured petals to attract insects. When an insect lands on a flower to drink nectar, it becomes covered in pollen from the stamen. Then, when the insect goes to another flower, the pollen from the first flower rubs off on the stigma of the second flower.

Pollination

When the pollen reaches the stigma, the plant is fertilised, and a tiny fruit or vegetable will begin to grow in place of the flower. This process is called pollination. Pollen can be carried from flower to flower by insects, the wind or by larger creatures such as birds.

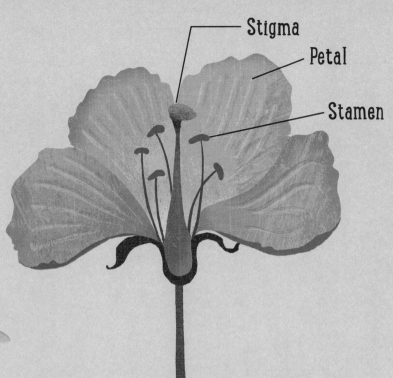

Stigma
Petal
Stamen

Bee friendly

Without pollination, we wouldn't have any fruits or vegetables at all! To be sure pollination will happen, our gardens must be insect-friendly places. Encourage insects into your garden or vegetable patch by planting flowers alongside your vegetables. Have a look in your garden and see how many bees and insects there are flying around.

Can you see the tiny vegetables beginning to grow?

What do plants need to help them grow?

It is very important that our plants get exactly what they need in order to grow. All plants need light, water, nutrients, warmth and air to grow properly. Let's have a closer look at what each of these does for our plants' growth.

Warmth

Plants need the right temperature in order to thrive – many more plants grow in the warm rainforest than in the freezing Arctic! If a plant is too cold, its tiny cells will crumble and break (test this out by putting some lettuce in the freezer); too hot and a plant will wilt, becoming limp. Many of the crops in this book should be planted once the weather has warmed up. Cold, frosty weather will kill them straight away. Seeds also need warmth to be able to germinate.

Light

Most of the vegetables in this book require sunshine. This is because plants can make their own energy using the power of the sun. Plants absorb the sun's energy through their leaves and, together with carbon dioxide from the air and water from the soil, make plant food from it. This amazing process is known as photosynthesis. A plant without enough light will struggle to grow properly.

Nutrients

Plants get nutrients from the soil, as well as through photosynthesis, so it is important to ensure that our soil is in good health. We also need these nutrients in our own diets to keep us healthy. We gain some of these nutrients through eating fresh fruit and vegetables.

Water

Plants must have water – they cannot grow without it. Water acts like a transport system to deliver nutrients around the whole plant. When your plants are full of water, they will look strong and healthy. Water helps to keep their leaves and stems stable and upright. If their leaves and stems are weak and floppy, it's a sign that they need watering. Many fruits and vegetables also need water to grow to a good size. Apples, pears and beans, for example, need extra water when their fruits are forming.

Soil and compost

The most important part of any garden is the soil. Without soil our plants would have nowhere to grow! All soil is slightly different. Some may contain more clay, making a heavy, thick soil that can be difficult to dig but holds on to nutrients. Sandy and silty soils are much easier to work with, but can dry out very quickly.

What is in soil?

- **Minerals** – these come from broken-down rocks and are essential for healthy plants.

- **Water** – water acts like glue and holds everything together.

- **Air** – there are lots of air pockets within soil, which allow water and oxygen to reach plant roots.

- **Organic material** – dead and rotting leaves, plants and wood.

- **Soil creatures** – soil contains millions and millions of tiny creatures. Some we can see, such as earthworms and beetles, while others, such as soil bacteria, are so small we can't see them. All these creatures do a very important job in breaking down the organic material.

Making a healthy soil

A healthy soil means healthy plants, healthy vegetables and therefore a healthy us! To make your soil healthier, it's a good idea to add plenty of garden compost to it. Garden compost is organic material that has rotted and broken down (see page 18–19). Compost gives the soil more nutrients.

What is garden compost?

Garden compost is a mixture of green and brown plant waste. Green waste is made up of soft green materials, such as vegetable peelings and tea bags, or grass and plant clippings. Brown waste is things like wood chip, cardboard and leaves. When these combine, together with warmth and moisture, they begin to decompose, which means they break down and turn into compost. Compost can be used to feed plants and soil.

How does waste decompose?

A compost bin is a living world. Inside there are millions of tiny creatures that turn the green and brown material into compost by breaking it down. Worms, ants and woodlice, as well as billions of bacteria and different fungi, all help to break down the material.

Ready to use

Compost is ready to use once it has turned dark black and crumbly, and you can't recognise any of the material that you put in it. During the summer, it can take as little as six weeks from start to finish. The process takes longer in winter, when it is colder.

Make your own garden compost

Have a go at making your own compost heap. It's as simple as creating a pile of your green and brown waste in an unused part of the garden. Turn it every 6 weeks to speed up the process.

However, to keep it tidy, ask an adult to help you fence it in using wooden pallets. Some local councils also supply compost bins. Once you've built your compost heap, watch it shrink as it starts to rot down. Make sure there is plenty of air circulation and that moisture can get in.

You can put almost anything on your compost heap, from teabags and egg shells to vegetable peelings and grass cuttings. Make sure you also add some brown waste such as scrunched up paper and cardboard. These create air pockets for bugs to move about in.

Tools and equipment

Every gardener needs the right tools and equipment to do the job properly. You can do most tasks using just your hands, but there are a few other important tools needed too:

Digging fork
A good, strong fork is essential for loosening the soil; it is also great for harvesting crops like onions and potatoes.

Spade
When it comes to digging larger holes, and trenches for crops like potatoes, a spade is the best tool.

Garden hoe
If you sow straight lines of vegetables, you can easily push a hoe between the rows to remove weeds.

String line
This can be just a piece of string tied in a straight line to two strong sticks. Although simple, it is an extremely useful tool for growing plants in straight lines.

Hand trowel and fork

Trowels are perfect for planting small plants into the garden or using to make a seed drill. A hand fork is the best tool for weeding your plot.

Other useful equipment

String, scissors, secateurs and a wheelbarrow are all handy to have, but are not essential.

Garden supplies

Other things that you may need include netting for protection from birds, and bamboo canes for building wigwams for bean and pea plants to grow up. You'll need to buy seeds and a bag of multipurpose compost. If you don't have them, you might also want to buy new pots and seed trays. There is a list of suggested seed varieties on page 106.

If you are going to buy new equipment, it's worth buying good quality tools so they will last for many years to come.

Preparing your vegetable patch

When the weather starts to warm up in spring, you can choose where you want to have your vegetable patch and what vegetables you want to grow.

Which position should you choose?

Vegetables like lots of sunshine. Try to choose an area that isn't shaded by trees or buildings. Watch the sunshine in your garden over the course of a day and look for the sunniest spots. These places will be good locations to grow your vegetables. You could use a compass to find out which direction your garden faces. A garden that faces south will generally get the most sunshine.

Making a vegetable patch

You can make your patch as big as you like, but remember that the more you take on, the more work there will be! A good size for a small vegetable patch is 1.5 m x 3 m. This should give you enough space to grow a number of different vegetables. Your patch could be part of an existing flowerbed or you could make one from scratch! Why not make a raised bed using timber planks as edges? Get an adult to help secure the planks to wooden posts at each corner.

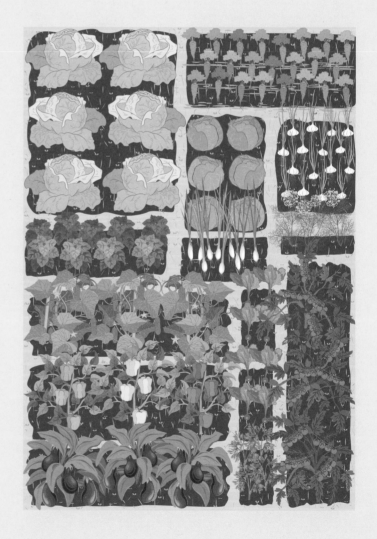

Preparing the soil

You will need to make sure that the area you choose is free from weeds. Use your hand fork to dig them up. Make sure you remove the roots or they'll keep growing back again.

When the area is clear of weeds, dig over the plot with your fork or spade. This will help to break up any hard soil and the roots of your vegetables will find it much easier to grow. Break up any big clods using the back of the fork.

Finally, use a rake to make sure the top of the soil is fine and crumbly. This will make it much easier to sow seeds and plant seedlings.

Sowing seeds indoors

Spring is the busiest time of year for a vegetable gardener. Many of our vegetables need to start their lives indoors. Spring is usually too cold to sow some delicate seeds, such as tomatoes and aubergines, outside. Starting to grow plants indoors means that you can control how much light, water and warmth your seedlings get. This will help them to grow into big and healthy plants once they are planted outside.

Pots and seed trays

For all of the seed sowing in this book you will need small pots and seed trays. There is a wide range of different pots and seed trays that you can sow your seeds into. Pots that are 9cm in diameter and plug seed trays are ideal for the job.

All of these pots and trays can also be made from everyday objects. Yoghurt pots, egg boxes and cardboard tubes make great pots. Whatever you use, put holes in the bottom for excess water to drain away.

Compost

It's always best to buy suitable compost to grow your seeds in. Multipurpose or seed compost will be free from weed seeds and diseases. It will also have the right amount of nutrients to feed your plants whilst they are young.

Where to grow them

At Kew Gardens we are lucky to have greenhouses where we can grow our seedlings. Greenhouses keep plants warm. At home you may also have a greenhouse or a conservatory you can use. Using a windowsill is just as good. You'll need to find one that gets plenty of sunshine throughout the day.

How to sow into pots

Fill each pot with seed compost. Level the compost with your hand, then give each pot or tray a few taps on the table. This will help the compost to settle. There should always be a gap of about 1cm at the top for when you water the seedlings. Otherwise the water will flow over the top of the pot and might take smaller seeds with it!

Take your seeds and place the required amount on top of the compost. Don't be tempted to sow the whole pack into one pot! They need to have enough space to grow.

Larger seeds can easily be pushed into the compost. Smaller seeds need to be lightly covered with a little more compost. Use another slightly larger pot as a sieve. Put a little compost into the bottom of the spare pot and gently shake it over the top of your seeds until they are covered. Water your pots.

Thinning out seedlings in pots

Once the seeds have germinated, you will have to remove any other seedlings to give enough space for one plant to grow on. This process is called thinning out. Sometimes it is possible to plant these extra seedlings into their own pot. Their roots and shoot will need to be intact. Make a hole in another pot of compost and drop it in.

Sowing into plug trays

1. Cover the whole tray with compost. Make sure every cell is full.

2. Level off the compost with your hand.

3. Use your finger to make a little hole about 0.5cm deep.

4. Now it's time to sow the seeds. If the seeds are small, such as lettuce or tomatoes, put 2 or 3 seeds into each cell.

5. For larger seeds, such as peas (shown) or beans, place the seeds on the soil and push them in.

6. Cover the seeds with more compost using a larger pot as a sieve.

7. To finish, water your seeds. You must use a watering can with a fine spray that won't drown or wash away your seedlings.

Label the pot with the date and name of what you have sown.

TIP!

To keep your seeds growing straight and strong you'll need to turn the trays around every couple of days. Keep pots and trays moist but not soaking wet.

Sowing and planting outside

Once the weather has warmed up in spring, seeds can be sown straight into the soil. Check that you can feel warmth in the soil. There should be no overnight frosts, and temperatures should be a minimum of 10°C. If it is too cold, your plants won't grow.

Sowing seeds outside

1. Use a string line to mark out where you want to sow your seeds. This helps you to sow in a straight line.

2. Make a seed drill. A seed drill is the name given to the shallow trench in which we sow our seeds.

   The depth of this will be different for each crop. You can use a garden hoe, a trowel, or simply your fingers to make a seed drill. Try to keep it the same depth all the way along.

3. Sow your seeds into the seed drill at the required distance apart. Carefully cover them with soil.

4. Water your seeds and watch them grow!

Thinning seedlings outside

It may be necessary to thin your crops. Each vegetable will be different but all require enough room to grow properly. The closer together they are, the smaller they will be. It may be hard to throw away young seedlings, but if you don't do this, your crops will compete against each other for light and nutrients. Then you will end up with fewer, smaller vegetables.

Hardening off

If you have grown plants from seeds in pots and trays inside, you must first harden them off. It can be quite a shock for young plants to be planted straight outside. To prepare them, they must be introduced slowly. Place them outside during the day and bring them in at night. Do this for about a week.

Planting out

Dig a hole roughly the same size as the rootball of the plant. Place the plant in the hole and fill the soil in around it and gently firm it in. Plants are very fragile when they are young, so make sure you don't pile the soil too high up against their stems, because this could cause rotting. Lightly water your plants and keep them moist during the first few weeks.

Everyday gardening tasks

Once your seeds and seedlings are in the ground, you need to take care of them. A big part of making your vegetable garden a success is looking after it as often as you can. By completing some simple, everyday jobs you will make sure you get the best harvests.

Watering

Your crops will soon let you know if they need water. Their leaves will droop and the plant will look limp. Most vegetables need watering at least twice a week. When the weather is hot and dry, you'll need to water them every day. Aim to get water to the roots, and keep the soil moist but not soaking wet.

Weeding

Weeds growing in your vegetable patch will compete with your crops for water, light and nutrients. Use a hand fork or a hoe to lift out the weeds, including the roots. You'll need to keep on top of this task as they can grow very quickly!

Fertiliser

Sometimes plants need a little help to get all the nutrients they need. Using fertiliser will help to make sure your plants are as healthy as possible. The easiest and most natural way to use fertiliser is to add well-rotted garden compost and manure to your soil. You can also scatter organic liquid fertilisers or plant food around the base of your crops. Always read the labels on the bottles carefully, and ask an adult to help.

Harvesting

An easy way to tell if your crops are ready to pick is to see if they are a similar size and colour to vegetables you would buy in the shops. If they're ready, then it's time to harvest and eat them! Crops such as beetroots, carrots and onions are picked only once. Vegetables such as runner beans, peas and courgettes will produce many crops. These need to be harvested almost every day during the summer months. Look for crops hiding away underneath leaves and make sure you pick them before they become too big!

Wildlife in the garden

Stop and look around your garden and you'll soon see that it's home to many creatures. From tiny insects, such as bumblebees and spiders, to much larger creatures such as foxes and birds. Many of our crops couldn't grow without some help from these animals.

Friends in the garden

Honey bees, bumble bees and other insects play a vital role pollinating many of our vegetable crops. Therefore it is important that we make our gardens a place they like to visit. Fill your garden with as many bee-friendly plants as possible, such as lavender and buddleia. You could also build places they like to live in. Why not try making a bee hotel out of old bamboo canes?

Worms are another essential creature. They help to break down our garden waste and leaves. Worms poo material that is perfect for a plant to take up through its roots! Worms also make lots of tunnels within the soil. These tunnels allow water and air to reach plant roots.

Ladybirds may look harmless, but they are very good at eating problem pests like aphids. A ladybird's young (which look completely different from ladybirds) also eat lots of aphids.

Other insects such as centipedes, hoverflies, spiders, lacewing larvae and wasps all eat insects that could potentially damage our crops. Encourage these insects wherever possible and they will keep the number of pests down.

Frogs, toads, birds and hedgehogs all love to eat some of the most troublesome pests in the garden … slugs and snails!

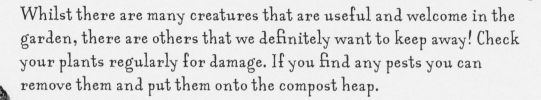

Garden pests

Whilst there are many creatures that are useful and welcome in the garden, there are others that we definitely want to keep away! Check your plants regularly for damage. If you find any pests you can remove them and put them onto the compost heap.

Slugs and snails are perhaps the most destructive pests in the garden. They can quickly munch their way through leafy crops, such as lettuce or cabbage. Encourage creatures such as blackbirds, frogs and toads that like to eat slugs and snails.

Move hungry *caterpillars* to the compost heap. It is worth covering any vegetables in the cabbage family, such as kale, cabbages or brussels sprouts, with fine netting. This will prevent the cabbage white butterfly from laying eggs on them.

Rabbits and deer are common pests in rural areas and can destroy all of your hard work very quickly! The only way to stop this from happening is to make a strong barrier, such as a fence, around your vegetable plot.

Birds such as pigeons can also eat your precious crops. At Kew, we put nets over many of our plants to stop the hungry pigeons.

Protect your small plants by covering with glass jars or the bottoms of plastic bottles.

Aphids are tiny insects that suck the sap, an important liquid containing nutrients, out of leaves and stems. They usually attack in large numbers. Try to wipe them off where possible or encourage ladybirds to eat the aphids. You can very gently move ladybirds from other plants in the garden to vegetables that have an aphid problem.

Diseases

There are also many plant diseases that can affect harvests. Fungal problems, such as potato or tomato 'blight', can destroy crops within a few days. You'll recognise blight as dark, rotting patches present on the leaves and stems of plants (see picture right). Unfortunately there is no way of treating the problem so as soon as you notice it, harvest any unaffected vegetables and dig up the infected plant. The fungus is blown around on the wind and splashed by raindrops, and therefore is usually a problem in wet, humid weather.

Powdery mildew (pictured left) is another fungus that attacks plants and can cause white, cloudy patches to appear on leaves. Plants such as peas and courgettes are prone to mildew attack. It can be difficult to prevent this but keep plants well watered and make sure they have enough space to grow properly. Crops planted too close together can be prone to fungal problems. Cut off any badly infected leaves.

Healthy eating

The food we eat, or our diet, is an important part of a healthy lifestyle. What you choose to eat can have an enormous impact on your energy and health. That is why it is important to learn how to eat well and make the right choices.

Nutrient rich

You can't see most nutrients, but they are, in varying amounts, in all foods. Fruit and vegetables, especially home-grown or organic vegetables, are some of the best sources of these healthy ingredients.

A rainbow of fruit and veg

Vegetables and fruit should form a large part of all of our diets. Every day, aim to eat a rainbow of different colours, textures and varieties. Brightly coloured raw vegetables are full of vitamins and minerals. The fresher they are, the more goodness there is inside them. Wash raw vegetables and chew them well.

Food groups

To have a balanced diet, we should aim to eat food from all five main food groups. Each food group contains different nutrients that work together to keep the body healthy. These groups are often shown on a 'food plate' that illustrates the proportions in which they should be eaten.

Fruit and vegetables keep our digestive system healthy. They are full of vitamins and minerals.

Carbohydrates provide us with energy. Bread, pasta and rice are carbohydrates.

Protein builds and repairs our bones, muscles, skin, hair and body tissues. Meat, fish, eggs and pulses contain protein.

Dairy products, such as milk, butter, yoghurt and cheese, help to build strong bones and teeth.

Fats keep us warm and can be stored in the body for energy. Foods that are high in fats, such as cakes, biscuits and crisps, should be eaten only in small amounts. Fats found in oily fish, olives, nuts and seeds are a healthier alternative.

Get ready to cook

Once you've harvested your vegetables, you'll want to start making some tasty dishes. But before you start cooking, there are some important things you need to know.

Be prepared

Make sure you have the ingredients you need for the recipe. You don't want to get half way through cooking to discover that you're missing a vital ingredient. Check that you have all of the equipment that you need too. Then you're ready to cook!

Ovens

Ovens should be preheated to the specified temperature. If you're using a fan-assisted oven, follow the manufacturer's instructions. Always ask an adult to help to turn the oven on for you and ask for help when using the hob. Use oven gloves when handling hot pans or baking trays.

Health and safety tips

1. Wash your hands with soap and warm water before you start.
2. Tie back long hair.
3. Rinse and dry all fruit and veg thoroughly.
4. Read through the recipe twice before you start cooking and check that you have all the equipment and ingredients to hand.
5. Immediately after preparing raw meat, remember to thoroughly clean everything that came in contact with it, such as the chopping board, knife, work surface and your hands.

Cooking equipment

Here are the most important tools and appliances we will be using in this book.

- An oven: for baking and roasting.
- A hob: for boiling, simmering and frying.
- A blender or food processor: for making purees, soups and pestos.
- A sharp knife: for chopping and slicing.
- A chopping board: essential for chopping and slicing on.
- A metal spatula: for scraping food off pans and trays and preventing food from sticking to them.
- A wooden spoon: for stirring.
- Medium, small and large mixing bowls.

- Weighing scales: it's good to have all the ingredients ready, weighed and laid out to hand.
- A garlic crusher.
- A masher.
- A sieve.
- A variety of cooking pans and trays: saucepans (large, medium and small), a large frying pan or wok.
- A casserole dish.
- A slotted spoon.
- Some tongs.

And of course, you will need an apron!

Growing carrots

There is nothing more satisfying than pulling up your own carrots straight from the soil. Their seed can be sown straight in the ground or in deep pots and containers. Sow from mid-spring to late summer.

Growing carrots in the ground

1. First prepare a seedbed using the instructions on page 28.

2. Use a string line to mark out where you want your row. Leave 30cm between rows.

3. Using a trowel, or your fingers, make a seed drill 2cm deep.

4. Carefully place a row of seeds into the drill, leaving a finger space between each seed.

5. Cover the seeds with soil and water them. Seedlings will appear in 2–3 weeks.

6. You'll need to make sure that each seedling has enough space. To do this, we use a process called thinning (see page 29). The aim is to give each carrot about 10cm of space. Keep the strongest seedlings and pull out the others.

7. Your carrots will be ready to harvest in 6–8 weeks. Hold their leaves and pull them gently from the soil.

Growing carrots in containers

It's easy to grow carrots in containers and this can give better results. Use a container that is at least 20–30cm deep. The container must have holes in the bottom so that excess water can drain away. Don't put too many seeds in one pot or the carrots won't have room to grow to full size. Pots dry out very quickly so check them daily to ensure they're still moist.

Carrot splitting

To make sure we get straight carrots it is important to check that the soil doesn't have any large stones. This could cause the carrot to split or 'fork' (see picture, left).

SOW OUTDOORS: March–July   HARVEST: May–Nov

Carrot colcannon

serves
4

2 large sweet potatoes

10g butter

1 large leek, sliced

salt and pepper

8 large carrots, peeled and sliced

12 rashers of streaky smoked
  bacon, cut into chunks

1 lemon, sliced in half

a drizzle of extra virgin oil

a knob of butter

1. Preheat the oven to 180°C (Gas Mark 4). Put a large pan of salted water on the hob to boil.

2. Wash the the sweet potatoes and bake in the oven for 45 minutes to an hour. You can check they are ready by poking them with a fork: if soft, they are cooked.

3. While the potatoes are baking, place a large frying pan on a medium heat and add the butter. Once melted, add the bacon and cook for a few minutes.

4. Stir in the leek and sprinkle with salt and pepper. Cook for 5–10 minutes, stirring often with a wooden spoon, until softened.

5. Meanwhile, place the carrots in the pan of boiling water and cook for 10 minutes until tender. Drain and mash them.

6. When the potatoes are cooked, cut them in half and scoop out the flesh. Add the flesh to the carrot and roughly mash them both together. Season with salt and pepper and the juice of half a lemon.

7. Add a knob of butter and a drizzle of olive oil, followed by the cooked leeks and bacon. Taste to check the seasoning. Add the juice from the other half of the lemon if you wish.

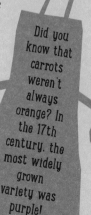

Did you know that carrots weren't always orange? In the 17th century, the most widely grown variety was purple!

Watch out for pigeons! They could eat all of your cavalo nero overnight; it may be wise to put some netting around your crop.

Growing cavolo nero

Cavolo nero is in the same family as cabbages and broccoli. We eat the leaves of the cavolo nero plant, which can be picked from late summer all the way through winter.

Sowing seeds indoors

In April, follow the instructions for sowing into pots or plug trays on pages 26–27. Sow 2 seeds per pot or cell. Once the seeds have germinated, pick out the weaker seedlings, leaving one in each pot. When the plants have reached 20cm in height, and they have been hardened off (see page 29), it's time to plant them out.

Planting out

1. Use a hand trowel to dig a small hole in the soil.

2. Place the plant in the hole. Be sure to firmly push the soil back in around the plant.

3. Give each plant plenty of space to grow. Around 45cm between each plant is ideal.

4. Water well in the first few weeks of growth and the plant will grow quickly.

5. Begin to harvest the leaves in the autumn. Pick a few small, tender leaves. Leave the smallest leaves at the top. They will be your next harvest.

SOW INDOORS: March–June PLANT: May–July HARVEST: Nov–Feb

Cavolo nero pesto pasta

serves
4

400g dried pasta
250g cavolo nero
60g basil
100g pinenuts
40g grated parmesan
1 garlic clove, crushed
4–5 tbsp olive oil
1–2 tbsp creme fraiche
juice of 1 lemon

1. Put a pan of water on the hob to boil, then add the pasta and cook for 8–10 minutes.

2. Meanwhile, wash the cavolo nero and strip the leaves from the tough stalks. Set the leaves aside and discard the stalks.

3. Bring another pan of water to the boil, add the cavolo nero and cook for 1 minute.

4. Drain the cavolo nero and, once it's cool, squeeze out as much water from it as you can.

5. Pick the basil leaves off the stalks and discard the stalks.

6. Put the basil and cavolo nero in a food processor along with the rest of the ingredients. Pulse until the mixture is smooth. This is your pesto mix.

7. Drain the cooked pasta and return back to the saucepan. Stir in the pesto and mix until completely combined.

8. Serve immediately.

Growing peas

Sow peas in early spring – they don't mind the colder temperatures. In around 3 months, your peas will start to produce pods – inside are peas, the sweetest vegetables in the garden and best eaten straight away!

Sowing seeds

1. Pea seeds can be sown directly into the ground in March, or you can start them in trays indoors. Follow the indoor sowing instructions on pages 26–27. Put one seed into each pot.

2. Place them outside off the ground or, for faster germination, on a windowsill.

3. Peas germinate and grow quickly. Once you can see the roots growing through the bottom of the pot, it's time to harden them off (see page 29) and plant them out.

Planting peas in a pot

1. Fill a large pot with multipurpose compost (you could use some garden soil first and then top it up with compost).

2. Using 4 bamboo canes (about 1.5m long), make a small wigwam. Get an adult to help tie it together at the top.

3. Plant the pea plants around the edge of the pot. They will need about 15–20cm of space between them.

4. The peas will need something to climb up. Tie some netting or twigs to the wigwam.

WATER & WATCH THEM GROW!

5. Look out for the pea flowers. When these fade away, the pea pods will appear and begin to swell. When they're nice and fat, they're ready to pick.

How do peas climb?

Peas have curly stems that they use to cling to structures. These are called tendrils. The plant uses these tendrils to climb and get closer to the light.

SOW: March–July PLANT April–June HARVEST: June–Oct

Pea gnocchi

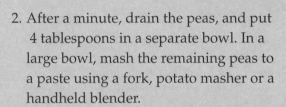
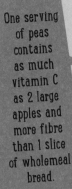

One serving of peas contains as much vitamin C as 2 large apples and more fibre than 1 slice of wholemeal bread.

serves 4

250g shelled peas

500g ricotta cheese

30g grated parmesan

1 egg

salt and pepper

125g plain flour

a few mint leaves

zest of half a lemon

juice of 1 whole lemon

drizzle of extra virgin olive oil

1. Place the peas into a heatproof bowl and cover them with boiling water to soften them.

2. After a minute, drain the peas, and put 4 tablespoons in a separate bowl. In a large bowl, mash the remaining peas to a paste using a fork, potato masher or a handheld blender.

3. Add the ricotta cheese, parmesan, egg and salt and pepper to the mashed peas. Mix well, then add the flour little by little, stirring slowly.

4. In a pan, bring some water to the boil. Roll a teaspoon-sized amount of gnocchi batter into a little ball in your hand, and place it gently into the water. You can cook about 12 at a time.

5. When the gnocchi float to the surface they are ready. Fish them out with a slotted spoon and place in a serving dish.

6. Spoon the peas you set aside earlier into the serving dish. Top with extra virgin oil and a generous squeeze of lemon juice. Garnish with a few mint leaves, lemon zest, black pepper and a grating of parmesan.

7. Serve immediately.

Growing lettuce

Lettuce is very quick and simple to grow. Seeds can be sown straight into the soil, but they also grow very well in pots and in windowboxes. Lettuce is crisper and sweeter eaten fresh.

Sowing

1. Place two lettuce seeds into each cell or pot, cover them over and water. Place on a sunny windowsill.

2. Once germinated, remove one seedling so there is one strong one left in each pot to grow on.

3. Be sure to harden off lettuces (see page 29) before you plant them out.

In early summer, seeds can also be sown straight into the soil outside.

Planting out

1. Your lettuces are ready to be planted out once you can see the roots growing through the bottom of the pot or tray.

2. Lettuce will grow well in a slightly shaded spot. Lettuces hate too much hot, bright sun and may 'bolt'. This means they will produce a flower stalk, which makes the leaves taste bitter.

3. Watch out for hungry slugs that love to eat lettuce! If this is a problem, grow lettuces in containers and place them off the ground. Why not try growing them in hanging baskets or in windowboxes instead?

4. Lettuces will be ready to harvest in about 8–12 weeks.

'Cut and come again'

Lettuce is known as a 'cut and come again' crop because most lettuce leaves can be picked and will grow back time and time again.

Lettuce scoops

serves **4**

3-4 heads of little gem or romaine lettuce

4 cans tuna steak

½ small red onion, finely chopped

a handful of fresh coriander

a handful of cherry tomatoes, quartered

4 tbsp crème fraîche

2 tbsp mayonnaise

2 tbsp capers

squeeze of lemon juice

a drizzle of olive oil

black pepper

1. Separate and wash the lettuce leaves, then carefully dry in a clean tea towel or salad spinner.

2. Drain the cans of tuna and put in a mixing bowl.

3. Finely chop the red onion and coriander and add to the tuna.

4. Add the cherry tomatoes, crème fraîche, mayonnaise, capers, lemon juice and olive oil to the bowl. Mix thoroughly. Taste to check the seasoning, adding more crème fraîche, olive oil or lemon juice if necessary.

5. Lay the lettuce leaves on their curved sides in a serving dish. Scoop a little of the tuna mixture into each salad leaf. Finish with a final sprinkle of pepper.

Lettuce belongs to the same family as the daisy and people have been eating it in salads for thousands of years.

Growing onions

Onions can be stored and used throughout the year. They are easy to grow either in large pots or straight in the ground. Onions can be grown from seeds in early spring. Or plant onions sets, which are small onion bulbs. You can buy onion sets from garden centres.

Growing onions

1. Use your string and pegs to mark out a straight line in the soil. Make a shallow drill or planting trench using a trowel.

2. Place your onion sets into the trench, making sure the root is at the bottom (the top will be much thinner).

3. Space the onion sets 10cm apart. You will need about 30cm between rows.

4. Press the soil back in around the sets so that just the wispy tops are showing. Initially it may be worth covering the sets with netting, because birds can often mistake them for worms!

Taking care of your onions

1. Keep the onions watered. Onion patches can become very weedy, so be ready to pull up any weeds that try to grow around your onions.

2. Harvest once the leaves die back and you can see the swollen onions in late summer. Use a fork to carefully lift them out of the soil.

3. Dry them out in the sunshine until their skins turn papery. One of the easiest ways to store onions is to put them in a net bag and hang them somewhere dry.

4. You could also try making an onion string. Twist each onion around a loop of string with the biggest at the bottom.

Medieval onions

In medieval times, bunches of onions were hung above doorways as this was believed to ward off diseases.

PLANT: March-April HARVEST: June-Sept

Onion soup

serves 2

1 knob of butter
2 tbsp olive oil
600g onions, sliced
1 leek, sliced
1 tsp sugar
salt and pepper
1.2l beef or vegetable stock cubes
2 garlic cloves, crushed
150ml red wine
1 small baguette
80g cheddar cheese, grated

1. Place the olive oil and butter into a very large, heavy-bottomed casserole dish on a low heat. Add the onions, leek, sugar, and salt and pepper, and stir with a wooden spoon to coat evenly.

2. Cook on the hob on a low heat, partially covered with a lid. Stir occasionally, until the onions are brown and sticky. This should take about 40–50 minutes.

3. Dissolve the stock cubes in 1.2l of boiling water.

4. Add the garlic to the cooking onions, then turn up the heat and add the wine. Let this cook for a few minutes, then follow with the stock.

5. Simmer, again partially covered with a lid, for 15 minutes.

6. When you are nearly ready to serve, slice the baguette. Brush olive oil over both sides of the slices and place on a baking tray. Cover each slice with grated cheese and place under a grill until melted.

7. Dish out your soup and pop a few slices of cheesy baguette on top. Enjoy!

Growing runner beans

Runner beans are hungry plants and will thrive in the garden, but you could also try to grow them in a large pot. Make sure you add some compost or manure. This will ensure the beans get all the food they need.

Sowing

Runner bean seeds can be planted straight outside. Push them into the ground about 2.5cm deep. You can also start them off inside. Follow the instructions on pages 26–27. Sow 1 seed per pot. You'll need 6 or 7 plants. Once they produce their first large leaves, harden them off ready to be planted outside.

Building a wigwam

Runner beans are climbing plants so, before we can plant, we must build them a wigwam.

1. You will need 7 long bamboo canes (2m long) and a 40cm length of string.

2. Make a rough circle in the soil with your finger, about 90cm wide.

3. Now push in the canes, evenly spaced, around the circle.

4. Get an adult to bunch the canes and tie them together using the string.

Planting

1. Dig a hole next to each cane. Place one plant by each cane.

2. Place your hand over the surface of the pot and turn it upside down – the plant will come away from the pot.

3. Put the plant in a hole and push soil around it to gently firm it in. Water well.

4. Once the beans start to form, they will swell quickly. Start harvesting once the beans reach 20cm. Any bigger and they'll taste tough and stringy.

Pests

Watch out for black fly – you can spray these off using a hose.

SOW INDOORS: April-June PLANT: May-July HARVEST: July-Oct

Runner bean and bacon spaghetti

400g spaghetti
2 tbsp olive oil
350g runner beans
12 smoked bacon rashers
1 tbsp fresh tarragon, finely chopped
40g parmesan, grated
1 egg, beaten
black pepper

1. Place a large pan of salted water on the hob to boil. When it's boiling, add the spaghetti and cook for 10 minutes.

2. Meanwhile wash, dry, then chop your runner beans into 1cm slanted chunks.

3. Put the olive oil in a large frying pan and place on a medium heat. Add the runner beans to the frying pan. Cook, stirring occasionally with a wooden spatula, for 6–8 minutes.

4. Chop the bacon into small chunks, and add to the pan along with the tarragon. Cook until the bacon goes a little brown and turn off the heat.

5. Drain the pasta once cooked but save a tablespoon of the cooking water. Add the spaghetti, water, parmesan and egg to the pan of bacon and runner beans and stir quickly for a minute.

6. Add plenty of black pepper and a grating of parmesan before serving.

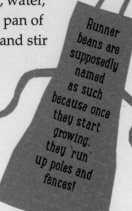

Runner beans are supposedly named as such because once they start growing, they 'run' up poles and fences!

In late summer to early autumn, your beans will be ready to harvest. Give the pods a shake. If you hear the beans rattling inside, they're ready to pick!

Growing borlotti beans

Borlotti beans have a beautiful and unusual pattern on their pods. Unlike French beans or garden peas, which are eaten fresh, we grow borlotti beans for their dried seeds.

Sow

In late April to May, follow the indoor sowing instructions on pages 26–27. You'll need 5 or 6 pots with 1 seed in each pot. Keep all seedlings well watered and they will germinate within a few days. Once they have grown their first two leaves, they are ready to be hardened off before planting out. You can also sow them straight into the ground.

Wigwam

1. With the help of an adult, construct a wigwam in the same way as for the runner beans on page 62.

2. Dig a hole next to each cane. Hold the base of the plant pot in one hand and tap the bottom of the pot to release the plant.

3. Place one plant beside each cane and press the soil firmly in around it.

4. Keep the plants well watered and watch as the beans grow and wind their way around the canes.

SOW INDOORS/OUTDOORS: April–June   PLANT: May–July   HARVEST: July–Oct

Borlotti bean burgers

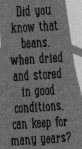

Did you know that beans, when dried and stored in good conditions, can keep for many years?

makes
4
burgers

600g fresh borlotti beans, pricked with a fork

1 baking potato

3 spring onions, chopped

8 sprigs of fresh coriander, chopped

1 egg

1 tsp cumin

1 tsp chilli flakes

salt and pepper

a bowl of sesame seeds

1. Preheat the oven to 180°C (Gas Mark 4).

2. Place the borlotti beans in a pan of cold water. Bring to the boil and cook for 20 minutes until tender.

3. Peel the potato and chop into four. Place the potato chunks in a pan of cold, salted water. Bring to the boil and cook for 10 minutes.

4. Drain the potatoes and mash. Add the borlotti beans and mash them both together.

5. Add the spring onions, chopped coriander, egg, cumin, chilli flakes and salt and pepper. Mix well.

6. Using your hands, divide the mixture into four. Flatten into burger shapes. It is fine if they feel quite wet. Roll them in the bowl of sesame seeds to coat and place them onto an oven tray covered with foil.

7. Bake for 40 minutes until nice and golden. Serve in buns with sliced tomato, lettuce and mayonnaise or the garlic dip (page 84), along with the polenta chips (page 89).

Growing tomatoes

Tomatoes aren't just red and round – they come in all sorts of shapes, sizes and colours, from deep purple to orange, yellow and even stripy green. Whatever type you grow, they're sure to taste delicious!

Sowing

Follow the instructions for sowing seeds indoors on pages 26-27. Sow 2–3 seeds per pot. Once germinated, remove the weaker seedlings to leave only one tomato plant per pot. When they reach a height of 20cm, they are ready to be hardened off (see page 29) and planted out.

Growing your tomato plant

Tomatoes hate the cold and will grow best in a warm, sunny environment. If you're lucky enough to have a greenhouse, this is the ideal place to grow tomatoes because it stays warm all day long. If you grow tomatoes outside, it is important that the weather is warm enough. Temperatures need to be above 10°C day and night.

When the weather is warm enough, transfer your plants from their pots to the soil outdoors. They will need around 40cm of space beside them. They can also be planted into grow bags or larger pots. Once they start to produce fruit, they will need bamboo canes or sticks to support them.

Tomatoes can benefit from an occasional liquid feed. Feeding will produce bigger and better tomatoes. Do this every week when the tomato plant starts to produce flowers and fruit.

Blight

'Blight' is a fungal disease that can attack the whole plant. Look out for black patches on the stem and leaves. If your plant has this, it's unlikely it will produce a good crop of tomatoes.

Pick the tomatoes as soon as they are bright red. The plant will keep producing more flowers and fruit through into the autumn.

SOW: March–April PLANT: MAY–June HARVEST: Aug–Oct

Tomato, feta and basil tart

1 x 320g packet of puff pastry
200g tomatoes
2 tbsp dijon mustard
a handful of fresh basil leaves
salt and pepper
1 tbsp feta
extra virgin olive oil
a little milk

1. Preheat the oven to 200°C (Gas Mark 6). Take the puff pastry out of the fridge. Remove the packaging but do not unroll the pastry. Leave it at room temperature for 10 minutes.

2. Carefully cut the tomatoes into slices.

3. After the pastry has been at room temperature for 10 minutes, unroll it on a baking tray whilst keeping it on the baking paper provided with it.

4. Roll each edge of the pastry in by 1cm to create a rim around the outside of the tart.

5. Prick the pastry base with a fork to stop the middle rising in the oven (you want the edges to rise to create a crust so don't prick those).

6. Using the back of a spoon, spread the mustard over the base of the tart. Arrange your tomato slices on top. Sprinkle with the feta, salt, pepper, olive oil and a few basil leaves.

7. Using a pastry brush, coat the tart edges with milk. Bake for 12 minutes, or until the pastry is crisp and golden.

When tomatoes were first brought to Europe in the 16th century, people were afraid to eat them because of their bright red colour usually associated with poisonous plants and fungi.

Growing potatoes

The excitement of digging up your own potato crop is hard to beat! Potatoes can be grown straight in the ground, in potato bags, or in large tubs. Whichever way, there is nothing better than digging up a fork full of golden potatoes straight from the soil.

Seed potatoes

Buy seed potatoes in late winter from a garden centre or nursery. Place the seed potatoes in an egg box and put on a windowsill. You will see that they begin to sprout, a process called chitting, which takes around 5 weeks. Sprouts need to be about 1cm before planting out.

Planting out seed potatoes

1. In late March to early April, choose a sunny position to plant your seed potatoes.

2. Using a spade, dig a trench 15cm deep and 20cm wide and as long as you have space for. Allow 60cm between rows.

3. If possible, place some garden compost in the bottom of your trench, which will help to feed the potato plants.

4. Place each seed potato in the trench, spacing them 30cm apart. Cover the seed potatoes with soil. Be careful not to damage the sprouts.

5. Once the potato plants have grown to 20cm, rake the soil up around the base of the plant. This is called earthing up; it will protect any potatoes growing near the surface and help to support the plant.

6. Keep an eye out for the flowers; they are very pretty and are a good sign that your potatoes are almost ready.

7. Use a fork to lift the potatoes and be careful not to poke any! Have a good dig around to make sure you get them all out of the ground.

Potato blight

Watch out for any black patches on the leaves and stems. This may be blight and could mean you lose your entire crop! Cut off any infected leaves and dig up any potatoes before it spreads to the whole plant.

PLANT: March-April HARVEST: June-August

Potato cakes

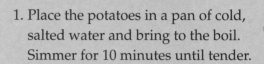

serves
4

600g potatoes, peeled and
   chopped into small chunks
6 tbsp finely grated parmesan
   cheese
4 tbsp plain flour
2 eggs
salt and pepper
10g butter
2 tbsp sunflower oil
Optional: 4 fried eggs

1. Place the potatoes in a pan of cold, salted water and bring to the boil. Simmer for 10 minutes until tender.

2. Drain the potatoes and then mash.

3. Add the parmesan, flour, eggs and seasoning, and mix well.

4. Place a frying pan on a medium heat and add the butter and sunflower oil.

5. When the butter has melted, add three or four (depending on the size of your pan) tablespoon-sized dollops of the potato mix. Flatten them using a spatula (you want the cakes to be fairly thin) and leave to cook for 2–3 minutes until golden. Flip them over and cook on the other side.

6. Once the first batch of cakes is done, add a little more sunflower oil or butter to the pan, and cook the next batch. Continue until you have used all the mix.

7. Serve the potato cakes with fried eggs for a scrummy breakfast or teatime treat.

Potatoes are one of the most complete vegetables to be found in terms of vitamin, protein and mineral content.

Watch out for birds that will want to eat your spinach. If birds are a problem, cover your crop with netting.

Growing spinach

Spinach leaves are tasty and very good for you. Young leaves are perfect for a salad or can be gently steamed. Spinach prefers to grow in the cooler temperatures of spring and autumn. It grows very quickly and can be cut again and again.

Sow new rows every 2–3 weeks and you'll have a continuous supply throughout the summer.

How to grow

1. Mark out a row with your string line. Leave 30cm between rows.

2. Make a seed drill about 3cm deep, using your fingers or a trowel.

3. Carefully place a seed every 3-4cm.

4. Gently cover the seeds with soil and water.

5. Leaves will appear in 2–3 weeks. They are ready to pick once 5–6 of the larger leaves have appeared. New leaves will appear and you'll be able to cut the leaves 2 or 3 times before the crop will finish.

SOW: March-Sept HARVEST: June-Nov

Spinach omelette

serves 4

500g spinach leaves
2 tbsp pinenuts
2 tbsp olive oil
1 medium onion, finely chopped
salt and pepper
¼ tsp grated nutmeg
8 eggs, beaten

1. Wash your spinach leaves and remove any tough stems. Dry your leaves using a clean tea towel or a salad spinner.

2. Place an extra-large oven-proof non-stick frying pan on a medium heat, and add the pinenuts. Lightly toast them without any oil for a few minutes. When most have turned golden, remove them from the pan and set aside.

3. Add the olive oil to the frying pan and, when hot, gently fry the onion for 2 minutes until translucent and soft.

4. Gradually add the spinach to the pan, using tongs to lift and toss them around until they are all wilted. Season with the salt, pepper and nutmeg. If there is more than a teaspoon of excess moisture in the pan, drain it off using a spoon.

5. Drizzle a tablespoon of olive oil around the spinach in the pan and increase the heat. Pour the eggs over the spinach and cook for 2 minutes, or until the eggs have set at the bottom and are still a little wobbly at the top. Use a spatula to lift the spinach and let the egg run underneath.

6. Spread the toasted pinenuts over the top of the omelette and finish under the grill for a couple of minutes until the top of the omelette has set.

Growing garlic

This rather smelly vegetable is used in many different recipes in the kitchen. It can be dried and stored so you can use it all year round!

Planting garlic

1. It is best to buy garlic bulbs from a garden centre to ensure they're healthy and free from disease. Separate the individual garlic cloves from the bulb.

2. Using your string line, mark out a straight line.

3. Use your finger to push each clove 5cm into the soil. The clove should have the wide root part facing down. Leave 15cm of space between each clove and 30cm between rows.

4. In a few weeks, small green shoots will emerge.

5. When the leaves start to turn yellow, use a fork to gently lift the bulbs out of the soil.

Rusty garlic

Watch out for rust – orangey brown spots that may appear on the leaves. There isn't much you can do about rust. If it gets too bad, covering the whole plant, then you can dig up the garlic early. It will just be smaller, but leave it to dry and you can still eat it.

PLANT: Oct-Feb Nov HARVEST: June-Sept

Garlic dip with crudités

serves 4

For the dip:
1 large garlic bulb
300ml greek yoghurt
salt and pepper
1 tsp ground cumin
juice of ½ a lemon

An assortment of vegetables
for dipping, such as:
  carrots
  celery sticks
  chicory
  cauliflower
  red pepper
  radishes

1. Preheat the oven to 140°C (Gas Mark 1). Place a whole, unpeeled garlic bulb on a baking tray and cook in the oven for an hour.

2. When the garlic is ready, remove from the oven and leave to cool for 5 minutes. Then, separate the cloves from the bulb and gently squeeze the cooked flesh out of the skins into a bowl.

3. Mash the garlic flesh, using a teaspoon or fork, until it is smooth. Add the yoghurt, salt and pepper, cumin and lemon juice.

4. Wash and chop your dipping vegetables (known as crudités) into sticks or bite-sized chunks.

5. Place the bowl of dip on a large serving plate, and arrange your chopped vegetables around it for easy dunking.

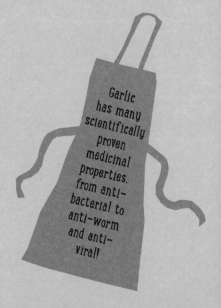

Garlic has many scientifically proven medicinal properties, from anti-bacterial to anti-worm and anti-viral!

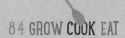

Growing courgettes

Courgettes belong to the same family as cucumbers, squashes and pumpkins. Just one or two plants will give you enough courgettes to last you right through the summer!

Growing courgettes

1. Start seeds off indoors in late April or early May. Sow one seed into 3 or 4 pots to ensure that you get at least 2 healthy plants.

2. Courgette seeds can also be sown straight in the ground. Sow seeds 2.5cm deep and leave at least 40cm of space between plants.

Planting out

1. If you started growing your plants indoors, harden the plants off (see page 29) once they have produced 4–6 leaves.

2. Dig a hole, using a trowel or spade, and plant. Make sure the soil isn't piled too close to the stem as this can cause it to rot.

3. Make a ring of soil around the plant. This will stop water running away and make sure it goes right down to the roots.

4. Courgettes are thirsty plants, so keep them well watered.

Harvesting

Be sure to harvest your courgettes when they are young and sweet (around 10–20cm). They grow so fast that they can quickly become too big. Check them every day throughout the summer.

Flower food

Did you know that courgette flowers can also be eaten? Deep fry them in batter for a delicious snack!

Courgette and polenta chips

serves 4

800g courgettes
100g polenta
50g parmesan cheese, grated
1 sprig of rosemary
200ml sunflower oil

1. Preheat the oven to 200°C (Gas Mark 6).

2. Wash the courgettes and chop them length and widthways into chip-sized sticks.

3. Put the polenta and parmesan in a bowl.

4. Strip the leaves off the sprig of rosemary and finely chop. Add to the bowl of parmesan and polenta and mix together.

5. Place the sunflower oil in a bowl. Dip each courgette chip in the oil and then coat them in the polenta mix.

6. Place the chips on an oven tray and bake for 25 minutes, or until golden.

Beware the giant in the garden: if left courgettes can grow to about a metre in size.

Growing chard

Chard is an amazing plant! It grows very quickly, can be picked continuously and will survive well into the winter months. It's also very tasty! Chard comes in an array of colours, from green, white and pink to deep reds and yellow. Growing chard will definitely bring a splash of colour into your vegetable garden!

How to grow

Chard can be sown directly into the ground in the same way as beetroots (see page 99). You can also sow chard seeds indoors from April to July. Sow 2 or 3 seeds into each pot.

When the seedlings have 2–5 leaves, it's time to plant them out. Remember to harden them off first (see page 29). Dig a hole in the soil, put one plant in and surround it with soil. The further apart you plant your seedlings, the bigger they will get.

Chard is one of the most nutritious vegetables that you can eat. It contains a high amount of vitamin K, which is important for helping wounds to heal.

Chard grows very quickly and after just a few weeks you will be able to start picking. Cut the stems near the base of the plant. Leave the very smallest leaves as these will be your next harvest!

SOW: April-Aug PLANT: May-Aug HARVEST: May-Nov

Chard noodle stir fry

serves 4

400g chard
1 white onion, chopped
2 tsp sesame oil
2 garlic cloves, finely sliced
1 thumb-sized piece of ginger, finely sliced
2 portions of straight-to-wok noodles
a drizzle of soy sauce
5 spring onions, finely chopped
1/2 lime
sesame seeds

1. Wash and dry the chard. Slice the stalk ends into little chunks and the leafy ends into strips.

2. Heat the sesame oil in a wok (or a very large, deep-sided pan) and add the chopped stalk ends and white onion. Soften for two minutes, stirring frequently, then add the garlic and ginger.

3. After 30 seconds, add the noodles and soy sauce. Use a wooden spoon or tongs to separate the noodle strands. Cook for 2–3 minutes, stirring all the time.

4. Add the sliced chard leaves and cook for 1–2 minutes to soften them. Continue stirring quickly.

5. Add the spring onions to the pan. Toss for a further 30 seconds.

6. Serve with a squeeze of lime juice and a sprinkle of sesame seeds. Eat immediately.

Growing aubergines

Did you know that aubergines come from the same family as tomatoes and potatoes? Aubergines like hot and humid conditions, so they grow well in greenhouses. However, they can also be planted outside if the weather is warm enough.

Sowing aubergine seeds indoors

1. Aubergines take a long time to reach their full size, so you'll need to plant seeds in late January or February.

2. Sow 2–3 seeds into 9cm wide pots.

3. Water and then place somewhere warm. Most windowsills will be fine for this.

4. After about 3 weeks, the seeds will start to germinate. Remove the weaker seedlings, leaving one strong plant in each pot.

5. Once the plants reach around 20cm, their roots will begin to run out of space in the small pot. Plant into a larger pot or plant outside, hardening them off first (see page 29).

Planting outside

It is best to wait until June or July to plant out so that the days and nights are warm.

1. Dig a hole big enough for your plant.

2. Put the plant in the hole and firm the soil around it. Leave at least 60cm between each plant.

3. Water well. In 3 or 4 weeks you will see flowers begin to develop. From these flowers your aubergines will grow!

WATER & WATCH IT GROW!

Eggplant

Ever wondered why aubergines are sometimes called eggplants? Aubergines can be black, purple or white, like an egg.

SOW: Jan-Feb PLANT: May-July HARVEST: July-Oct

Aubergine rounds with tomato topping

serves 4

3 aubergines

2-3 tbsp olive oil

150ml Greek yoghurt

1 lime

250g cherry tomatoes

½ garlic clove

salt and pepper

1 tbsp extra virgin olive oil
  (for the tomatoes)

6 sprigs of coriander, chopped

1. Preheat the oven to 180°C (Gas Mark 4).

2. Wash, dry, then slice the aubergines widthways into 1cm thick rounds.

3. Place the olive oil in a small bowl, then, using a pastry brush, cover both sides of each round with olive oil.

4. Bake in the oven for 30 minutes or until golden. Halfway through cooking, turn them over to cook both sides evenly.

5. Meanwhile, place the yoghurt in a bowl and squeeze over the juice of half a lime. Crush the garlic and add to the yoghurt with a pinch of salt and pepper. Taste to check the seasoning.

6. Quarter the cherry tomatoes then place in a bowl and drizzle over the extra virgin olive oil and a squeeze of juice from the remaining lime half.

7. Arrange the cooked aubergine on a serving plate and dollop over the yoghurt, then the tomatoes, then the coriander. Enjoy!

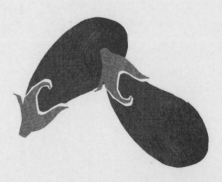

Beetroots can be purple, white or yellow.

Growing beetroot

Beetroot is one of the easiest vegetables to grow in the garden. Not only do we eat the root part of the plant, but the young leaves are also delicious.

Sowing beetroots

1. Make a seed drill about 2 or 3cm deep.

2. Place the beetroot seeds individually into the drill, about 3 or 4cm apart.

3. Cover the seeds with soil and water. Keep the ground moist as the beetroots grow.

4. When the seedlings emerge, it is important to give them enough space to grow to a good size. Each beetroot plant will need around 10–15cm of space. Choose which ones you want to keep and remove the other seedlings in-between. You could make a measuring stick to use as a spacer.

5. Harvest your beetroots when they are the size of a golf ball.

SOW OUTDOORS: March–July **HARVEST:** June–October

Beetroot chocolate loaf

serves 8

100g milk chocolate, melted

1 large beetroot

200g butter, at room temperature

200g sugar

3 eggs

200g plain flour

75g cocoa powder

1 tsp vanilla extract

1 tbsp maple syrup or honey

pinch of salt

1. Preheat the oven to 180°C (Gas Mark 4).

2. Take a loaf-shaped tin and coat the insides with butter. Then line it with greaseproof paper.

3. Break the chocolate into small pieces and put into a heatproof bowl. Place the bowl over a small saucepan of simmering water on the hob. Make sure the bottom of the bowl doesn't touch the water. Let the chocolate slowly melt.

4. Wash the beetroot and trim off any scraggly bits. Using a cheese grater, grate the whole beetroot, skin included. Wash your hands to stop them staining red.

5. Beat the butter and sugar in a mixing bowl, stirring quickly with a wooden spoon until creamy. Add the eggs. Gently stir in all of the remaining ingredients (including the melted chocolate) until combined.

6. Pour your gooey chocolatey mixture into your loaf tin. Bake in the oven for an hour.

7. Using oven gloves, remove the cake from the oven. After 5 minutes, gently remove the cake from the tin, and leave to cool on a rack.

It is a very good idea to wear an apron when cooking with beetroot. It contains the pigment betalain which can be used to dye fabric!

Growing chillies

Chillies have a hot and spicy flavour.
Grown at home, they will do best in a
very warm position like a greenhouse
or a conservatory. A hot windowsill,
or perhaps a very sunny spot in your
garden, is also good.

Growing from seed

1. Chillies need a long growing
   time before they produce fruit,
   so sow seeds early in the year.
   Sow 3-4 seeds in each pot.

2. Place the pots somewhere
   warm, such as a well-heated
   room or even an airing
   cupboard. The seeds need lots
   of heat and moisture.

3. In 2–3 weeks, the seeds will
   begin to germinate. Use a
   pencil to help you carefully
   remove the weaker seedlings
   in the pot, leaving just the
   strongest one.

4. Move the pots into a space
   where they will get lots of light,
   such as a windowsill.

Growing the chilli plants

1. Once the chilli plants reach a height of 20cm, move them into a bigger pot or plant them outside in a warm, sunny position. June is a good month to plant them outside as all risk of frosts has now passed.

2. Leave at least 40cm between each plant.

3. Water regularly, especially in summer.

Choose a mild type of chilli to grow (see varieties on page 106). Some types can be very hot and irritate your skin. If you choose to grow a hot variety, then it's a good idea to wear gloves when handling them.

Mexican spice

Did you know that chillies originally come from Mexico in Central America?

SOW: Jan–Feb PLANT: May–July HARVEST: July–October

Chilli hot chocolate

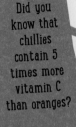

Did you know that chillies contain 5 times more vitamin C than oranges?

serves
2

600ml semi-skimmed milk
1 chilli
2 tbsp cocoa
1 pinch of cinnamon
2 tsp sugar

1. Put the milk in a small saucepan and place on a very low heat.

2. Using a sharp knife, make a little cut lengthways in the chilli. If you want only a little hint of spice, make a smaller cut.

3. Place the chilli in the milk pan. The spice will infuse in the milk. Wash your hands thoroughly. Chilli can really sting if it gets near your eyes.

4. When you see little milk bubbles at the edge of the pan, add the cocoa and cinnamon. Use a wooden spoon or whisk to stir.

5. Add the sugar to the pan and stir well. Carefully taste a little to check you are happy. If it's not spicy enough, then leave it to infuse for a bit longer.

6. When you're happy with the taste, place a tea strainer over a mug and carefully pour in the hot chocolate. The strainer will catch the chilli. Wait a few minutes for the drink to cool, then enjoy.

Further information

Growing varieties

Carrot: For a tasty, fast-growing carrot try 'Early Nantes'. 'Chantenay Red Cored' are small carrots great for growing in pots. For something totally different try the completely purple carrot, 'Purple Sun'.

Kale: 'Nero di Toscana' produces upright dark green leaves – delicious!

Pea: For a fast crop of peas that will be ready by early summer, give 'Feltham First' a try.

Lettuce: Crisp and sweet 'Little Gem' is the perfect little lettuce. Alternatively the spotted 'Freckles' will give colour to a salad bowl.

Onions: Try the traditional white onion 'Stuttgart Giant', which stores well into the winter months, or the dark crimson 'Red Baron'.

Runner Beans: 'Scarlet Emperor' produces an abundance of tasty, long beans. Keep picking and they will keep growing!

Borlotti Beans: For a striking bean worth having in any vegetable plot, 'Fire Tongue' is hard to beat.

Tomato: 'Red Alert' is a bush tomato perfect for growing in pots. It produces masses of sweet fruits long before most other varieties.

Potato: You can buy first earlies, second earlies or main crop potatoes. First earlies are the quickest to mature and take around 100 days from planting until harvest. Try 'Red Duke of York', a lovely red potato, perfect for any use in the kitchen.

Spinach: 'Amazon' and 'Palco' are quick to grow and can be picked time and time again. 'Perpetual' spinach will grow well into the winter months.

Garlic: 'Early Purple Wight' produces purple-tinged garlic bulbs. Or you could grow the enormous but milder-tasting 'Elephant Garlic'.

Courgette: Yellow and green varieties are available, such as 'Atena' or 'Defender'. You could also plant round types, such as 'Summer Ball', which you harvest when they are the size of tennis balls.

Swiss Chard: 'Bright Lights' will give a splash of colour to your garden including yellow, pink and white stems.

Aubergine: 'Money Maker' will grow better outside than some other varieties and can produce plenty of flavoursome deep-purple fruits.
Beetroot: 'Detroit 2' is a calssic purple beetroot. You could also try 'Golden', a deep-coloured, yellow beetroot that taste great when roasted. 'Chioggia' are sweet and have a wonderful striped pattern within.
Chillies: 'Padron' peppers are mild and delicious grilled. Be careful to select chilli varieties that aren't too hot, such as 'Cayenne Sweet'.

Supplier list

Seeds, small vegetable plants and gardening equipment can be brought from most local garden centres or nurseries. For a wider choice try buying online.

The Organic Gardening Catalogue
Superb range of certified organic seeds and plants and they offer a great range of child-sized tools and equipment. **www.organiccatalogue.com**

Thompson and Morgan
Excellent range of seeds and fruit trees, many of which are perfect for growing in small spaces. **www.thompson-morgan.com**

Thomas Etty
They sell a wide range of heritage seed varieties that have been grown for generations. **www.thomasetty.co.uk**

Suttons Seeds
A wide selection of equipment for growing your seeds and plants into.
www.suttons.co.uk

Sarah Raven
An easy-to-use and attractive website with lots of ideas for your garden.
www.sarahraven.com

Sow Seeds
This company has excellent vegetable seed collections, notably a 'Sow fun Children's Vegetable Seed Collection'. **www.sowseeds.co.uk**

Glossary

aphid a small insect that eats by sucking the juices of plants

bacteria tiny single-celled creatures that can help to break down living things

blight a plant disease that destroys parts or all of a plant

bulb the rounded part of the plant that begins to grow below ground

flower the part of a plant that has petals and makes fruit and seeds

clay a thick heavy soil

decompose to rot and break down

diet the food or drink usually eaten or drunk by a person

fertilisation the successful coming together of male and female cells

fruit the part of a plant that holds the seeds

fungi organisms that help to decompose dead plants and animals

garden compost made up of garden and kitchen waste. Compost is added to soil to provide nutrients for plants.

germination the process when a seed begins to sprout and grow

hardening off to put plants outside for a few hours each day to get them used to colder temperatures before they are planted out

leaves the parts of a plant that absorb energy from the sun to help them photosynthesise

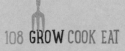

mildew a powdery fungus that grows on plants

nectar a sweet liquid produced by a plant that attracts insects

nutrient something that helps people, plants and animals to live and grow

organic material dead and rotting leaves, plants and wood found in soils

pod the long, thin pouch that contains seeds of a pea or bean plant

pollen tiny yellow powder made by a flowering plant

pollination the spread of pollen from one flower to another so it can make seeds

root the part of the plant that usually grows underground

sap the liqud that carries nutrients and water to all parts of a plant

seed the small part of a flowering plant that can grow into a new plant

seed drill a small trench in which seeds are sown

shoot the new growth of a plant

stamen the male part of the flower

stem the main structure of a plant that supports the leaves, flowers and fruit

stigma the female part of the flower that receives pollen

soil the top layer of earth in which plants grow

thinning out to remove weak seedlings from a pot or the soil to ensure
that strong seedlings will have enough space to grow

Index

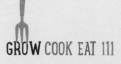

Conversions and abbreviations

The following abbreviations have been used in this book:

Abbreviations		Weights				Liquids/volumes	
tbsp	tablespoon	15g	½ oz	200g	7 oz	100ml	3½ fl oz
tsp	teaspoon	20g	¾oz	250g	8 oz	150ml	¼ pt
ml	millilitre	25g	1 oz	300g	10 oz	200ml	7 fl oz
l	litre	50g	2 oz	350g	12 oz	300ml	½ pint
g	gram	75g	3 oz	400g	14 oz	400ml	14 fl oz
cm	centimetre	100g	4 oz	500g	1lb	500ml	17 fl oz
m	metre	175g	6 oz	1kg	2lb	600ml	1 pint
						1 litre	1¾ pint

All eggs are medium unless stated.

Acknowledgements

The Publishers would like to thank the following for their help with this book:
Susan Allan, Tom and Josh Martin, Isabella and Mia McGregor, Lily and Polly Munson, Cerys and Liam O'Sullivan, Zachary Pang, Ruth Thomas, Olivia Walker

The publishers would like to thank the following for their kind permission to reproduce photographs:
Kew planting photography: Thom Hudson, apart from: 8 top, 43 middle, 47 bottom, 55 bottom, 59 top, 71 top, 74 bottom, 75 top, 94 bottom, 96 middle and bottom, 99 bottom by Joe Archer © The Board of Trustees of the Royal Botanic Gardens, Kew 2016

Recipe photography by Ian Garlick © Wayland 2016

All remaining photographs from Shutterstock: 8 bottom left: Africa Studio; 8 right: C Levers; 9 top: Normal Chan; 9 middle left: Pixeljoy; 9 bottom: Kostiantyn Kravchenko; 11 top: Petr Baumann; 11 bottom: Bogdan Wankowicz; 12 top: showcake; 12 bottom: TippaPatt; 13 bottom left: Sergej Razvodovskij; 13 bottom right: Bahadir Yeniceri; 12 middle: Honey bees: Peter Waters; 12 Bumblebee top left: hsagencia; 18 left Bernatskaya Oxana; 18 middle Gerald A. DeBoer; 19 top: Evan Lorne; 19 bottom: Marina Lohrbach; 20 middle: johnbraid; 22 fresher; 32 top Boonroong; 32 bottom StevenRussellSmithPhotos; 34 top Jiri Hera; 34 top left Sarah2; 34 top right Alexander Raths; 34 bottom TwilightArtPictures; 35 top dabjola; 35 middle Vadym Zaitsez; 35 bottom Julie Vader; 36 bottom kazoka; 38 Antonio Danna; 50 top oksana2010; 55 top Dieter Hawlan; 55 middle: rodimov; 71 middle Anna North; 74 top Swellphotography; 79 top Nataliia Melnychuk; 86 top Eag1eEyes; 90 top Kanjanee Chaisin; 90 bottom Arena Photo UK; 94 top Nataliia Melnychuk; 96 left Sarin Kunthong.